HOW TO
EAT A
LOBSTER

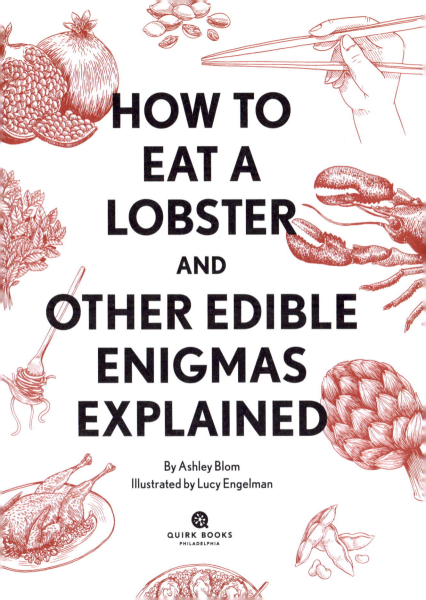

HOW TO EAT A LOBSTER

AND

OTHER EDIBLE ENIGMAS EXPLAINED

By Ashley Blom

Illustrated by Lucy Engelman

QUIRK BOOKS

PHILADELPHIA

Text copyright © 2017 by Ashley Blom
Illustrations copyright © 2017 by Lucy Engelman

Library of Congress Cataloging in Publication Number: 2016941165

ISBN: 978-1-59474-921-6

Printed in China

Typeset in Cervo Neue and Nobel

Designed by Andie Reid
Production management by John J. McGurk

Quirk Books
215 Church Street
Philadelphia, PA 19106
quirkbooks.com

10 9 8 7 6 5 4 3 2 1

TO MY MOM

Thanks for supporting me
through the years. I'll never
forget the time you were
worried I'd mess up cooking
dinner for the first time, but
then you proceeded to set the
taco shells on fire yourself.
I love you.

CONTENTS

Introduction ··· 9

TRICKY TECHNIQUES

How to Eat a Whole Fish ··· 12

How to Eat a Lobster ··· 16

How to Eat Crawfish ··· 21

How to Eat Raw Oysters ··· 24

How to Eat Escargots ··· 26

How to Eat Bugs ··· 28

How to Eat Asparagus ··· 30

How to Eat an Artichoke ··· 32

How to Slice an Avocado ··· 34

How to Open a Coconut ··· 38

How to Pick Out Ripe Fruit ··· 42

How to Eat Edamame ··· 44

How to Eat Kohlrabi ··· 46

How to Slice a Mango ··· 48

How to Eat a Papaya ··· 51

How to Eat a Pomegranate ··· 53

How to Eat a Rambutan ··· 55

How to Eat Kumquats ··· 58

How to Go Nuts ··· 60

How to Eat Durian ··· 66

How to Carve a Chicken ··· 68

How to Eat a Quail ··· 71

How to Eat Pigs' Feet ··· 73

How to Eat a Pig's Head ··· 75

ETIQUETTE ENIGMAS

How to Use the Correct Fork ··· 80

How to Use Chopsticks ··· 84

How to Taste Cheese ··· 86

How to Eat Noodles ··· 90

How to Sip Soup ··· 92

How to Hold a Wineglass ··· 95

How to Taste Wine ··· 98

How to Make a Toast ··· 101

How to Drink Tea ··· 104

How to Use Bread as
a Utensil ··· 106

How to Eat Sushi ··· 108

How to Tip ··· 111

How to Decide Who Pays
the Bill ··· 114

How to Order from the
Menu ··· 116

How to Excuse Yourself
from the Table ··· 120

FOODIE FIXES

How to Eat Something
Spicy ··· 126

How to Eat Something
Messy ··· 127

How to Pace Yourself
When Drinking ··· 129

How to Stay Vegetarian
at a Barbecue ··· 132

How to Stick to Your Diet
at a Party ··· 135

How to Fix Bad Breath ··· 138

How to Handle Beans ··· 140

How to Taste Something
You Hate ··· 142

How to Recover from
a Tongue Burn ··· 144

How to Send Food Back ··· 146

How to Stop Yourself
from Choking ··· 148

Resources ··· 150

About the Author ··· 154

About the Illustrator ··· 155

Index ··· 156

Acknowledgments ··· 160

INTRODUCTION

Imagine this: You're in polite company—perhaps a business lunch, a fancy dinner party, or meeting your future spouse's parents—and suddenly there's a whole fish on the plate in front of you. Or maybe the cooked foot of a pig. Or maybe the only utensil offered is a pair of chopsticks or a loaf of bread. Are you prepared? Do you know what to do? Or do you excuse yourself, escape to the coat check, dig out your phone, and frantically research how to properly, and politely, consume your unexpected dinner?

Honestly . . . do you even know how to excuse yourself from the table? There are etiquette rules for that!

Where is that coat check ticket, anyway?

Stop. Put the phone away. You got this.

The following tips and tricks will explain, step by step, how to navigate these and many other edible enigmas with poise and grace. Whether your dinner is staring back at you or it's your turn to set the table, you'll know just what to do and how to do it.

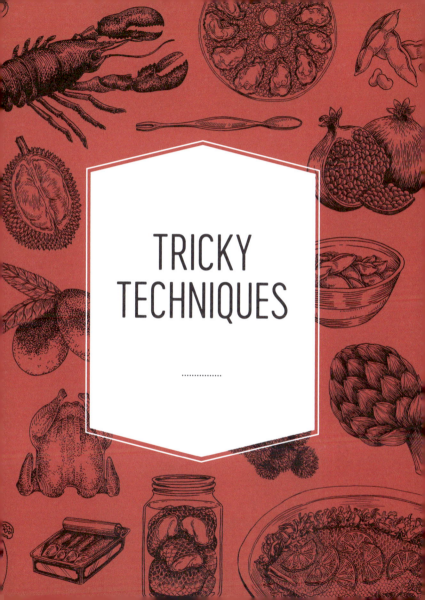

TRICKY
TECHNIQUES

....

EAT A WHOLE FISH

Does your dinner have a face? Follow these steps and you won't regret it the staring contest. The flavor punch of a whole fish is more than worth it.

YOU WILL NEED

Whole, cooked fish

Knife (ideally a fillet knife, but any small sharp knife will do)

Fork or spoon

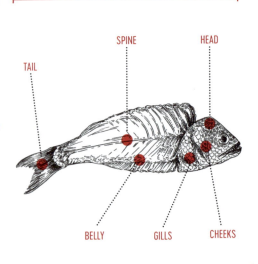

TAIL

SPINE

HEAD

BELLY

GILLS

CHEEKS

STEP 1 If the fish is small, like a sardine, the bones are edible and you can eat it whole. Something like pickled herring can also be eaten whole because the vinegar in which the fish is stored softens the bones. If confronted with a larger fish, proceed to step 2.

STEP 2 With the knife, make a cut just behind the head, parallel to the gills, just deep enough that the knife hits the spine. Make a second cut just in front of the tail, again not all the way through the body, stopping at the spine.

STEP 3 Make a cut parallel to the belly, right below the spine.

STEP 4 Use a knife or fork to gently push the meat off the ribs from the spine down to the belly.

STEP 5 Remove the backbone by lifting the tail and pulling the spine up and off the body. Use the knife to extract any visible bones left in the meat.

STEP 6 You should now have a boneless fillet on your plate. Slice off the head and tail and discard them, or scoop out any meaty bits you find in the head. Serious seafood foodies highly recommend fish cheeks.

TIP Alternative Method: Properly cooked fish will flake off the bone. If you don't mind a mess, you can simply use a fork to remove the meat from the body.

— FISH ALERT! —

Whole fish is popular in many cultures and restaurants. You're most likely to encounter it in a stew, encased in a salt crust, or grilled. Luckily, menus usually indicate that a fish will be served whole.

> **❝It was always the biggest fish I caught that got away.❞**
>
> EUGENE FIELD

EAT A LOBSTER

Once considered a poor man's food, lobster now graces the tables of the rich, the famous, and the vacationing masses. Here's how to disassemble this bottom-dweller with ease.

YOU WILL NEED

1 whole, cooked lobster

Lobster cracker, nutcracker, or scissors (this may not be necessary if the shells are soft)

Bin for discarded shells

Plastic bib with a lobster on it (required attire)

Lobster fork (optional)

Butter for dipping (optional)

STEP 1 Locate the edible portions of the lobster:

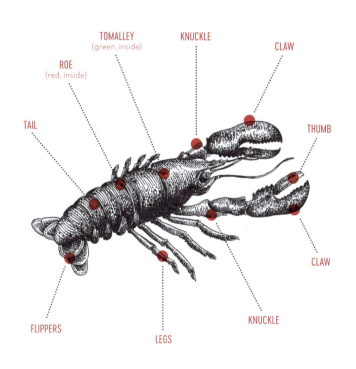

TOMALLEY
(green, inside)

KNUCKLE

CLAW

ROE
(red, inside)

THUMB

TAIL

CLAW

FLIPPERS

LEGS

KNUCKLE

STEP 2 To remove the tail, grasp it with your hand, gently twist, and pull it off the body.

STEP 3 Pull the flippers off the end of the tail. Push your finger or lobster fork through the opening, working the tail meat out the other end. Discard empty shells in the bin.

STEP 4 Find the digestive tract: the dark gray line running through the tail. It is safe to eat, but it doesn't taste very good. Remove it.

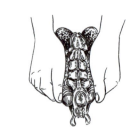

STEP 5 Twist off the claws and knuckles. Pull the thumb off each claw and discard it; the meat should be left in one piece on the rest of the claw.

STEP 6 Use the lobster cracker to crack off the top third of the claw. Pull out the meat with the lobster fork. Dip meat into butter. Consume ravenously.

You may stop here or join the legions of serious lobster eaters and continue on to the body of the beast.

STEP 7 Peel the outer shell off the body with your hands; it should come off fairly easily.

STEP 8   There is a bit of soft white meat between the inner gills of the lobster. Use a pick or small fork to gently pull it out.

STEP 9   Next, look for the bright red roe, which will be present in female lobsters. This is considered a delicacy by lobster lovers.

STEP 10   Finally, if you feel like taking a chance, scoop out the green tomalley, aka the liver. Because the liver filters out toxins, it is not always recommended eating, but lobster aficionados claim it's the best part. You can eat it by the spoonful or spread it on crostini.

LOBSTER ALERT!

Lobster is most common in coastal areas, where it is available fresh. You are most likely to encounter a Maine lobster, the type with large claws and tail, as described here. Rock lobsters, which can be found in warmer waters, do not have large claws and typically only their tail is served. Lobsters are cooked by steaming or boiling, and occasionally they're stuffed with a mixture of bread crumbs and seafood (typically crab).

EAT CRAWFISH

These small, tasty crustaceans, sometimes called mudbugs, look like miniature lobsters. They are often boiled with a hefty pour of Cajun spices. If your Southern host dumps a pile of them in front of you, don't fret. Shelling them is easier than you'd think.

YOU WILL NEED

Crawfish

Bucket for discarded shells

Butter or remoulade for dipping (optional)

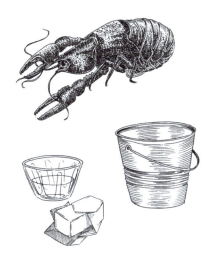

STEP 1 With one hand, pinch the crawfish by its head. With the other, pinch the spot where the tail meets the body.

STEP 2 Twist the tail and pull it away from the body. Optional step for the non-squeamish: suck the juices from the head, and then discard it. (See "Crawfish Alert!" on page 23.)

STEP 3 Twist off the tail flippers. Devein the crawfish (its dark, stringy digestive tract should come off easily).

STEP 4 Gently use your thumbs and forefingers to work off the first two or three rings of the wider part of the shell. Pull out the exposed tail meat. Dip the meat into butter (if desired), and enjoy.

 TIP If the crawfish is relatively big, you can eat the claw meat as well. Crack the shell with your hands or by biting it in half. Use a small fork or a piece of shell to scoop out the meat.

CRAWFISH ALERT!

Crawfish live in fresh water. You're certain to find them in the southern United States, especially Louisiana. The juices from the head could very well be a pure shot of Cajun spices if your host is a fan of spicy foods. Skip this step if you can't handle the heat.

EAT RAW OYSTERS

Yes, oysters are alive when you eat them. They will be served with their shells cut open and nestled on a bed of ice with condiments on the side. They should be wet, with a bit of liquid in the shell. Master this skill and you're sure to impress your friends.

YOU WILL NEED

Oysters on the half shell

Oyster fork

Condiments such as lemon wedges, horseradish, hot sauce, or shallot vinegar (optional)

STEP 1 Order some oysters. They are typically served in singles, by the dozen, or by the half dozen.

STEP 2 Use a fork to gently pry the meat from the shell, being careful not to spill the juices.

STEP 3 For your first taste, skip the condiments. You'll want to experience the full flavor of the oyster before you decide if it needs a little boost.

STEP 4 Lift the shell to your lips and tip the oyster and its juices into your mouth.

STEP 5 Experts and foodies agree that you should chew the oyster a few times to release all the flavor. If you're not big on strange textures, you may prefer to swallow the whole mouthful in one go.

— OYSTER ALERT! —

You may have heard the old rule to "only eat oysters in months that end in 'r,'" but in modern times, thanks to year-round farming, oysters are safe to eat anytime. However, due to oysters' natural spawning cycle, you will find the tastiest morsels in the spring. If buying oysters to shell at home, pick ones that are heavy for their size.

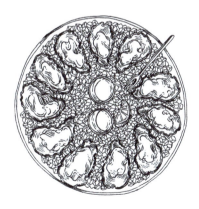

EAT ESCARGOTS

Enjoying these spiral-shelled delicacies is a sure-fire
way to feel very cultured and French.

YOU WILL NEED

Escargots (cooked snails)

Escargot tongs

Escargot fork

Butter or sauce for dipping
(optional)

STEP 1 With your nondominant hand, use
the tongs to pick up a single snail shell.

STEP 2 With your dominant hand, use the
fork to pierce the meat and pull it out of the
shell.

STEP 3 Dip the snail in the provided butter
or sauce (if desired). Eat the entire mouthful
at once. Do not nibble it!

 Escargots will be served on a snail plate,
which has little wells for the shells. The
butter or sauce will be either directly on
the snail or served on the side for dipping.
If escargot tongs and special fork are not
provided, use a napkin (never your bare
hands!) to pick up the shell and a regular
fork to pull out the snail.

── **ESCARGOT ALERT!** ──

Escargots are available fresh year-round. You're most likely to be served ones that have been boiled and then baked or broiled. Take the opportunity to taste the history—snails have been on the menu for millennia. The ancient Romans loved them, and evidence of people eating snails has been found in prehistoric sites.

EAT BUGS

The edible insects you'll most likely encounter in the U.S. are prepared ants and crickets, but in other countries you may find yourself with a plate full of beetles or tarantulas. Go for it! It's just protein, right?

YOU WILL NEED

Prepared bugs, such as ants, crickets, beetles, or tarantulas

STEP 1 Remove sharp extremities such as spiny legs, stingers, or fangs.

STEP 2 If the bug is alive, bite off the head firmly and quickly. This will ensure that the bug does not struggle in your mouth.

STEP 3 Eat the bug whole, and chew well.

 Preparation is everything. If the idea of crunching on a live cricket gives you the heebie-jeebies, seek out cooked bugs that are flavored with ingredients you enjoy. For example, look for chocolate-covered ants or seasoned earthworms. If you want to start with a low-stakes taste, try cricket flour, a common ingredient in high-protein diets.

Entomophagy (*noun*):
the practice of eating insects

EAT ASPARAGUS

You have two options for consuming this vegetable: using your fingers or your cutlery. Follow your host's lead.

YOU WILL NEED

Cooked asparagus spears

Knife

Fork

Dipping sauce

Plate for discarded stalk bases (optional)

The Modern Way

If you are served long spears that have not been cut prior to serving, you may wonder exactly how to consume them without looking like a cow chewing cud.

STEP 1 Pierce the spear with a fork to hold it in place.

STEP 2 Use a knife to gently cut the spear into bite-sized pieces. If the base of the spear is tough and does not yield to gentle pressure, set it aside. Don't eat it.

STEP 3 Pierce one piece with the fork and dip or drag it in the provided sauce. Eat.

The Old Way

Victorian high-society etiquette stated that asparagus is a finger food. If you are served spears sans silverware or are engaging in time travel, here's how to proceed.

STEP 1 Pick up the spears, one at a time, by the base. Use only your fingertips.

STEP 2 Dip a spear into the provided sauce, and eat from top to bottom. (It goes without saying that Victorian ladies would not approve of double dipping.)

STEP 3 Discard the tough base onto a separate plate.

EAT AN ARTICHOKE

Some say the artichoke is the perfect excuse to consume a bowl of butter free from criticism. Others say, "How the heck do you eat this thing?"

YOU WILL NEED

A fully cooked artichoke

A small bowl of butter seasoned with lemon or aioli

STEP 1 Check the artichoke for sharp barbs at the top of each leaf. Typically, these are removed prior to cooking, but if they are still intact, proceed with caution.

STEP 2 Starting at the bottom of the artichoke bulb, gently pull off a leaf. If the artichoke has been cooked properly, the leaf should come off easily.

STEP 3 Hold the top of the leaf and dip the bottom two-thirds in butter.

STEP 4 Don't eat the whole leaf—it will be too tough to chew. Instead, use your teeth to gently scrape the soft flesh off the leaf. Discard the rest of the leaf.

STEP 5 Repeat with the rest of the leaves. Inside the artichoke are underdeveloped barbs. Scrape these out with a spoon or fork and discard.

STEP 6 Eventually, you will reach the heart of the artichoke, where the leaves are soft. Eat the heart in full, with a hefty dab of butter, of course.

SLICE AN AVOCADO

Creamy and rich, with a mild nutty taste, the humble avocado is a true thing of beauty and a nutritional powerhouse, packed with vitamin K, fiber, folate, and healthy fats.

YOU WILL NEED

Avocado

Sharp knife

Cutting board or countertop

Spoon (optional)

STEP 1 With a sharp, nonserrated knife, cut lengthwise into the avocado. You will feel the knife stop at the pit. Keeping the knife in place, hold the avocado in your palm and slowly turn it around the knife in a circular motion, cutting the avocado in half around the pit.

STEP 2 Remove the knife and twist the halves in opposite directions. They will come apart easily, and the pit will be in one of the halves. Place the pit half on a cutting board or countertop. Quickly hit the center of the pit with the heel of the knife. The pit should come out easily on the knife. If it resists, press the knife into the pit as shown. Pick up the avocado half in your nonknife hand and carefully twist the fruit while holding the knife steady.

STEP 3 Cut the flesh into slices or a cross-hatch pattern.

STEP 4 Turn the skin inside out, and the flesh should fall out. If any pieces stick to the skin, use a spoon to gently scoop them out.

TIP To check if an avocado is ripe, use a fingertip or fingernail to gently pop off the stem and look inside. If the flesh is light green, it is ready to eat. The fruit will yield when you squeeze it gently. If the stem doesn't come off with light pressure, the avocado is not ripe. A few ways to ripen an avocado: 1. Set it on a sunny windowsill. It will ripen over the next few days. 2. Put it in a brown paper bag with an apple. The bag will trap the ethylene gas given off by the apple, which speeds ripening. 3. Bury it in flour inside a brown paper bag. It should ripen within 3 days; check it daily. If you plan to reuse the flour, wash and dry the avocado before burying it; after removing the avocado, sift the flour.

In the United States, avocado consumption peaks over Super Bowl weekend. The Hass Avocado Board estimates that about 278 million were consumed during the week before the 2016 game.

OPEN A COCONUT

Reenact your favorite stranded-on-a-desert-island movie
from the comfort of your own home.

YOU WILL NEED

Coconut

Skewer

Towel or dishcloth

Mallet

Kitchen knife

Butter knife

Paring knife

STEP 1   Locate the "eyes" of the coconut—the three dots on the top—and poke until you find two that give to gentle pressure. Push them in with the skewer.

STEP 2   Drain the liquid into a bowl or jar and chill. (Coconut water is a great source of electro-lytes and tastes good, too.)

STEP 3   Hold the coconut in one hand with the towel. Using the mallet, firmly tap it on all sides while turning, until the shell cracks.

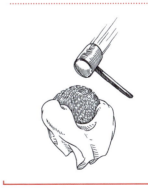

STEP 4 Use the kitchen knife to pry the two halves apart.

STEP 5 Use the butter knife to slice the white flesh and separate it from the shell. Use a paring knife to peel the brown skin from the flesh. Serve.

TIP How to Open a Coconut in the Wilderness: So long as you have a sharp knife or machete, you can open a coconut. Locate the seam between the eyes and use the knife to chop right into the seam. The coconut should come apart and the meat can be scooped out as above. If you want to reserve the juice, chop off just the top of the coconut and drain before cutting further.

COCONUT ALERT! ────────

You're likely to find fresh coconuts year-round, but especially from October through December. Choose a heavy one. You should be able to hear the liquid inside when you shake it, but the eyes shouldn't be leaking.

"For a moment, or a second, the pinched expressions of the cynical, world-weary, throat-cutting, miserable bastards we've all had to become disappears, when we're confronted with something as simple as a plate of food.**"**

ANTHONY BOURDAIN IN *KITCHEN CONFIDENTIAL*

PICK OUT RIPE FRUIT

**Follow these tips to choose perfect,
ready-to-eat fruit every time!**

Berries: Look for bold, brightly colored fruit. If white or green spots are visible, the berry was picked before it reached peak ripeness and should be avoided. Overripe berries may be mushy or brown.

Stone fruits, mangoes, and avocados: Hold the fruit and gently press it with your thumb. If the fruit gives slightly, it is ripe enough to eat. If it is too hard, it is not yet ripe. If it is too soft or the skin breaks, it is too ripe.

Melons: Knock your knuckles on the fruit. If the sound is low and hollow, it is ripe. If it is shallow and hard, the fruit is not yet ripe. Ripe melons should give only slightly when pressed; if the melon gives easily, it is overripe.

Bananas and plantains: A banana with bright yellow skin is ready to be eaten; some people prefer a fruit with a few brown spots. Plantains can be eaten at every stage of the ripening process, from green to very dark brown or black.

Always try to buy fruit that is in season and native to your area. Fruits that have to travel long distances are typically picked before peak ripeness and may not ripen sufficiently in the store.

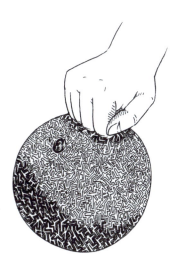

EAT EDAMAME

These fresh green soybeans are usually served in their fuzzy pods, with anything from a sprinkle of salt to more complex seasonings. Get ready to use your hands.

YOU WILL NEED

Cooked edamame pods

Napkin

Bowl for discarded empty pods

STEP 1 Roll up your sleeves, if necessary, and keep a napkin nearby to wipe your fingers after eating.

STEP 2 Hold an edamame pod with your fingertips, placing your fingers on either side of the seam at the top of the pod.

STEP 3 Bite down gently on the pod to open it, and use your teeth to pop the beans into your mouth. If the pods are flavored, suck off a bit of the seasoning.

STEP 4 Discard the empty pod.

**"Kids are now eating things like edamame and
sushi. I didn't know what shiitake mushrooms
were when I was 10—most kids today do."**

EMERIL LAGASSE, QUOTED IN *FOOD & WINE*

EAT KOHLRABI

A farmers market staple, this green root vegetable tastes similar to celery root, broccoli, and cabbage.

YOU WILL NEED

Kohlrabi root

Sharp knife

Kitchen shears

Vegetable peeler (optional)

Mandoline slicer (optional)

STEP 1 Using the sharp knife, make cuts across the top and bottom of the bulb. Snip off the greens with the kitchen shears. (Save these. They are delicious when sautéed.)

STEP 2 Using the knife or peeler, peel off the tough outer skin. Discard the skin.

STEP 3 Stand the bulb on the flat bottom and slice it in half from top to bottom. Cut each piece in half so you have 4 quarters.

STEP 4 Use the tip of the knife to cut out the tough core. Discard it.

STEP 5 Cut the quarters into matchsticks or discs, or slice thinly with a mandoline (especially if using the kohlrabi in a salad).

STEP 6 Use the pieces to make slaws and salads, or cook them as you would any root vegetable.

┌─────────────── **KOHLRABI ALERT!** ───────────────┐

If you receive a farm share basket or CSA, you're likely encountering this weird-looking member of the cabbage family on a regular basis. They're easy to grow and mature in less than 12 weeks, so many farmers take advantage of the hearty bulb, which can be eaten raw or cooked. The leaves are edible, too, and taste like turnip greens.

└───┘

SLICE A MANGO

Mangoes have a wide, flat, centrally located seed that can be challenging to remove if you don't know what you're doing.

YOU WILL NEED

Mango

Sharp nonserrated knife

Spoon (optional)

STEP 1 Locate the small bump on the mango, also called its eye. The seed is behind the bump, so you'll cut around it. Place the fruit on a cutting board with the bump facing up.

STEP 2 Insert the knife blade into the mango about a half inch to one side of the bump. Cut down along the center to the bottom, slicing off one side. If the knife hits the seed, continue cutting a bit closer to the skin. Repeat on the other side of the mango. You should have three pieces: two skin-on slices and the middle containing the seed.

STEP 3 Scrape out the flesh with a large spoon. Alternatively, you can cut a checkerboard pattern into the fruit and turn the skin inside out over a plate. With a knife or spoon, scrape off the flesh that remains around the seed.

Mango are harvested twice per year, so you're likely to find them in stores year-round. Ripe mangoes will be mostly red and yellow and give slightly when pressed. These juicy tropical fruits are good eaten fresh, made into smoothies or desserts, or used in salsas.

EAT A PAPAYA

Enjoy a taste of the tropics by dissecting this exotic fruit.

YOU WILL NEED

Papaya

Cutting board

Sharp nonserrated knife

Metal spoon

Melon baller (optional)

STEP 1 Place the papaya on the cutting board and use the knife to slice off about a half inch from each end. Be gentle; a ripe papaya's flesh is very soft.

STEP 2 Slice the papaya in half lengthwise.

STEP 3 Use a spoon to scoop out the seeds and the strands they're attached to.

STEP 4 Cut the papaya into smaller sections and carefully remove the skin with the knife. Alternatively, you can use a melon baller to scoop the flesh out of the skin.

If you don't live in a tropical area and you're not on a cruise, you're probably more likely to encounter papaya flavoring or papaya juice rather than fresh papaya. But don't let that stop you; the juice is a delicious source of vitamin C. And if you do have access to the fruit, dig in. It's juicy and sweet.

❝There is no love sincerer than the love of food.❞

GEORGE BERNARD SHAW

EAT A POMEGRANATE

In Greek mythology, Persephone ate six pomegranate seeds and was stuck in Hades every winter. Perhaps if she'd known how to prepare the fruit herself, she could have avoided that whole mess.

YOU WILL NEED

Pomegranate

Sharp knife

Bowl of water large enough to submerge the pomegranate

STEP 1 With the knife, slice about a half inch off both ends of the pomegranate.

STEP 2 Make vertical cuts in the skin just deep enough to break through the skin.

STEP 3 Submerge the fruit in the bowl of water and pull it apart at the cuts.

STEP 4 Pull the seeds out of the white pith with your fingers. The seeds will sink to the bottom of the bowl and the pith will float to the top.

STEP 5 Discard the pith and strain the seeds from the water. Eat the seeds whole.

TIP To freeze pomegranate seeds (also called arils), first let them dry thoroughly. Then spread them on a baking sheet and place the sheet in the freezer. When the seeds are completely frozen, put them in an airtight bag, seal tightly, and return to freezer until ready to use.

— POMEGRANATE ALERT! —

Pomegranate pros: Its sweet-tart flavor is unparalleled. The fruit—protected by a leathery skin—is generally available in the United States between August and December. It's high in vitamin C, vitamin K, folate, and dietary fiber. Pomegranate juice is also commercially available and is an easy way to enjoy the fruit's taste without the work of cutting and cleaning. Pomegranate con: Be forewarned . . . pomegranate stains.

EAT A RAMBUTAN

Rambutans may look like tiny torture devices, but fear not! The spikes won't hurt you, and the fruit inside is soft and sweet.

YOU WILL NEED

A rambutan

Small paring knife

STEP 1 Use the paring knife to gently slice about halfway around the center of the fruit, pressing down just hard enough to break through the skin.

STEP 2 Gently pinch the fruit on either side and pull the halves apart. The white globe should pop out easily.

STEP 3 Use the paring knife to cut into the center of the fruit. Pry out and discard the seed. Pop the fruit into your mouth and enjoy!

 TIP If removing the seed with a knife is too much work, you can eat the fruit whole and work the seed out in your mouth. In polite company, however, the knife method is preferred.

RAMBUTAN ALERT!

Rambutans are a common snack in Asia, where they are typically eaten plain. Their taste and texture are similar to lychees, but a bit more sour. The flesh is used to make jellies, salads, and ice cream. Rambutans don't ripen after being picked, so make sure that the fruit you select is brightly colored (typically red, but there are some yellow varieties) and not leaking juice.

EAT KUMQUATS

Kumquats are a small, sour citrus fruit cultivated in the United States, China, and Japan. They look something like miniature oranges, but you can eat the skin, which tastes sweet.

YOU WILL NEED

Fresh kumquats

STEP 1 Don't peel the fruit; there's no need. This should go without saying, but do wash them. Always wash the skin of any fruit you eat or cut through.

STEP 2 Pop a kumquat into your mouth, skin and all.

STEP 3 Chew, swallow, and enjoy.

❝I hate people who are not serious about meals. It is so shallow of them.❞

OSCAR WILDE IN *THE IMPORTANCE OF BEING EARNEST*

GO NUTS

Nuts are a portable, filling snack, but which ones require a nutcracker? Which are sold toasted? Here's what to know.

YOU WILL NEED

Assorted nuts

Nutcracker

Hammer

Nutpick

Bowl for discarded shells

Almonds

These teardrop-shaped nuts are the most widely cultivated in the world; they are typically available raw or toasted, either whole, sliced, or in pieces. To peel, blanch in boiling water, pat dry, and gently squeezenuts out of their brown skins with your fingers.

Brazil Nuts

A staple of the mixed-nuts medley, Brazil nuts are big, sweet, and rich and can be eaten raw or roasted. You can buy them shelled or unshelled. To shell, crack with a nutcracker, but note that the shell is extremely thick, so make sure your nutcracker is up to the task! One pound unshelled is equivalent to 3¼ cups shelled.

ALMONDS

BRAZIL NUTS

CASHEWS

CHESTNUTS

HAZELNUTS

MACADAMIA NUTS

PEANUTS

PECANS

PISTACHIOS

WALNUTS

Cashews

Because their shells are toxic, these C-shaped nuts are usually sold shelled. Whether raw or toasted, they are delicious eaten out of hand. They're also a popular ingredient in Indian, Chinese, Thai, and other recipes.

Chestnuts

Technically chestnuts can be eaten raw, but you're more likely to run across them roasted, candied, boiled, or incorporated into a recipe. Their bitter skins and hard shells will already have been peeled, or they will be served with the shell cracked open enough that the meat can be pulled out.

Hazelnuts

Also called filberts, these sweet round nuts are a favorite for baking. They're also found raw in nut mixes, toasted and sprinkled over vegetables, and of course in Nutella, the chocolate-hazelnut spread.

Macadamia Nuts

Macadamias have very hard shells, so they're most often sold shelled, either raw or roasted. They're large, white, sweet, and rich. Eat them out of hand or use them in baking recipes.

Peanuts

Yes, they are technically legumes. But you'll find peanuts sold with the nuts, shelled or unshelled, roasted or raw. To shell, hold one between both thumbs and first fingers. Pull apart the halves and gently squeeze each side until the nut pops out. Rub peanuts between your fingers to remove the skins. One pound unshelled peanuts is equivalent to 2 ⅔ cups shelled.

Pecans

Most famous for starring in rich pies, pecans are delicious in a range of sweet and savory dishes, not to mention raw as a snack. To shell, first sort and discard any that rattle when you shake them. Boil them in a large pot of water for 10 to 15 minutes. Drain and let cool. Place a nut between the handles of a nutcracker and squeeze gently until the shell cracks. Rotate it and squeeze again. Repeat until the shell comes off. Clean nuts carefully, and let them dry in a strainer for 24 hours before eating or cooking with them. One pound unshelled is equivalent to 2 cups shelled.

Pistachios

These delicately flavored pale-green nuts are a holiday staple. Pistachios are typically sold roasted. After roasting, the shell should be slightly open; use your fingers to pry apart the two halves and eat the meat inside. A completely closed shell, is a sign that the nutmeat is immature; discard it. If the shell is open but not open wide enough for you to pry apart, take a discarded shell from another pistachio, push it into the opening, and turn it like a key. The halves should come right apart. One pound unshelled is equivalent to 3 ¼ to 4 cups shelled.

Walnuts

You can buy walnuts in their shells or shelled. They're delicious in baked goods or toasted and then sprinkled over salads. If you find them unshelled, get ready for a challenge—they're notoriously tough. Place them in hot water and let them soak for 24 hours to soften them. Place one, pointed end up, on a hard surface and hit the point with a hammer. Then pull the shell apart. Use a nutpick to loosen the nut from the inside of the shell and pop it out. Heads up: walnut hulls will stain your hands black. Consider wearing gloves, and cover your clothing, work surface, nearby children, and anything else you might touch while working. One pound unshelled is equivalent to 2 cups shelled.

Toasted Nuts

Toasting nuts gives them a deeper, roasted flavor. Arrange nuts in a single layer on an ungreased baking pan or rimmed baking sheet. Bake in a 350°F oven for 5 to 10 minutes, stirring occasionally and watching carefully to make sure they don't burn. When they become fragrant, use a spatula to transfer the nuts from the baking pan to a bowl or plate to cool. Even a little extra time on the hot pan could cause them to burn.

Nuts in their shells are typically much less expensive than their shelled counterparts. The extra weight of the shell rarely cancels out the savings.

Frozen Nuts

Freeze nuts, shelled or unshelled, that you won't eat or use right away to keep them fresher longer. Here's how long they will last in the freezer:

Almonds	9 months
Brazil nuts	9 months
Cashews	9 months
Chestnuts	9–12 months
Hazelnuts	9 months
Macadamia nuts	9 months
Peanuts	6 months
Pecans	12 months
Pistachios	12 months
Walnuts	12 months

NUTS ALERT!

A few rules apply to all nuts: Buy them as fresh as possible. Unshelled nuts should have no cracks or holes and be heavy for their size. Shelled nuts should look uniform in color and size. Store nuts in an airtight container in a cool place to keep them from going rancid.

EAT DURIAN

This huge, brownish-green fruit native to Malaysia is known throughout Southeast Asia as the "king of the fruits." It is covered in spikes and has been said to smell like anything from gasoline to rotting meat. But its rich, creamy texture and sweet, buttery taste make the experience worthwhile.

YOU WILL NEED

Durian

Large, sharp knife

Cutting board

Spoon

STEP 1 Place the durian stem side down on the cutting board.

STEP 2 With a large knife, make a deep cut about halfway from the top down into the fruit, creating a hole large enough to stick your fingers into.

STEP 3 Using your hands, pull apart the skin to reveal the creamy yellowish fruit inside. It should break in half. If the skin is too hard to pull apart, cut it a bit more or ask a strong friend to assist you.

STEP 4 Scoop out the fruit pods with a spoon and enjoy! Be careful to avoid the hard brown pits.

DURIAN ALERT!

To describe durian as huge is not an exaggeration. This fruit can weigh up to 10 pounds! Look for it in Asian markets in the United States. In Southeast Asia, durian is sold in grocery stores and by street vendors. Wherever you buy fresh durian, don't transport it on public transportation or in other enclosed spaces.

❝They said that if you could hold your nose until the fruit was in your mouth a sacred joy would suffuse you from head to foot that would make you oblivious to the smell of the rind, but that if your grip slipped and you caught the smell of the rind before the fruit was in your mouth, you would faint.❞

MARK TWAIN

CARVE A CHICKEN

"Would you like to carve?" they asked. "Sure," you said.
"Can I take that back?" you thought when the chicken came
out of the oven. Don't panic. Here's what to do.

YOU WILL NEED

Whole roasted chicken

Large cutting board

Sharp carving knife

Large serving plate

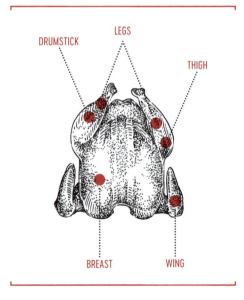

DRUMSTICK

LEGS

THIGH

BREAST

WING

STEP 1 Place the chicken on the cutting board, with the breast (the large curved side) facing up. If it has just come out of the oven, let it rest for at least 10 minutes.

STEP 2 Remove the legs: Hold a leg with one hand. Hold the knife in the other hand and position the blade where the thigh meets the breast. Wiggle the knife slightly to find the joint where the thigh is attached. Press the knife hard on the joint to separate the leg from the body. Repeat with the other leg.

STEP 3 Separate the drumsticks and thighs: Locate the joint that connects the thigh to the drumstick. Press hard on the joint with the knife to separate them. Repeat with the other leg. Transfer the drumsticks and thighs to a serving plate.

STEP 4 Remove the wings: Locate the joint connecting one wing to the body and press on it with the knife to cut off the wing; repeat on the other side. Transfer the wings to the serving plate.

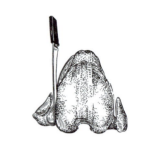

STEP 5 Remove the breasts: Cut down the center of the chicken, stopping when you feel resistance from the breast plate. Slide the knife horizontally down either side, cutting each breast off in one long motion. Slice meat to the desired thickness and transfer to the serving plate.

 TIP Don't throw away the bones! Place them in a large stock pot with celery, carrots, onions, garlic, parsley, peppercorns, and just enough water to cover everything. Bring to a boil over high heat, lower heat to medium-low, and let simmer for 2 hours. Strain out the solids and refrigerate the liquid overnight. The next day, use a spoon to skim off the fat. Store the stock in the freezer until you need it.

EAT A QUAIL

Quail is perfect for anyone who has dreamed
of eating a whole chicken in one sitting.

YOU WILL NEED

Whole cooked quail or
other small game bird

Dinner plate

Sharp knife

Fork

Carve as you would a chicken (see page
68) on your dinner plate instead of a large
cutting board. In short:

STEP 1   Place the quail on the dinner plate
and hold it steady with the fork in the center
of the breast.

STEP 2   Remove the legs and wings by
cutting through the joints with the knife.

STEP 3   Cut down the center of the breast,
using the breast plate as your guide.

STEP 4   Make a vertical cut down either side
of the breast to remove the breast meat.

QUAIL ALERT!

Quail is typically served whole, occasionally wrapped in bacon or prosciutto. If you're served quail at a fancy dinner party, proper etiquette is to use a knife and fork to get as many morsels off the bones as possible. At a more casual event, however, eating quail with your hands is perfectly acceptable. Game hens are slightly bigger, and the same rules apply (though the knife-and-fork method is easier with these larger birds).

EAT PIGS' FEET

If you can eat a hot dog, you can eat a pig's foot.

YOU WILL NEED

Cooked pig's foot

Knife and fork,
or your hands

Think of a pig's foot like a bigger, porkier chicken wing. If cooked properly, the meat should fall off the bone easily. There are no standard etiquette rules about how to eat pigs' feet, so assess your company and select your strategy:

- **Silverware strategy:** Use the fork and knife to work the meat off the bone and eat it.

- **By-hand strategy:** Pick up the entire foot and bite the meat off the bone.

"Fools make feasts, and wise men eat them."

BENJAMIN FRANKLIN

EAT A PIG'S HEAD

Go whole hog and dine on this lesser-used part of the pig.

YOU WILL NEED

Whole cooked pig's head

Large cutting board

Damp towel (optional)

Fork

Sturdy, sharp boning knife

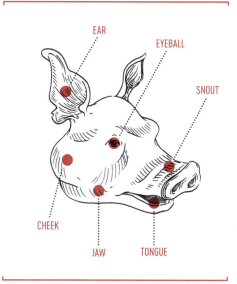

EAR

EYEBALL

SNOUT

CHEEK

JAW

TONGUE

STEP 1 The head will likely be served either split (cheek side up) or whole (chin on the plate). Nearly every part of the head is edible, including the tongue, snout, and eyes, so extracting the meat can begin anywhere. The biggest pieces are the cheeks and the areas around the jaw, eyes, and ears. Place the head on a cutting board (covered with a damp towel if desired).

STEP 2 Cut off the ears where they connect to the head by placing the knife behind each ear and slicing it off. These can be eaten whole.

STEP 3 If the pig has been cooked properly, the cheeks can be pulled from the bones with just a fork. Cut through the skin with the knife, starting just below the top of the ear, where the fleshy cheek bulges out to the side. Slice the meat off the head.

STEP 4 Use the knife to slice off sections of meat from under each eye. Use a fork to remove pieces the knife can't reach. If you're feeling adventurous, stick the knife into the side of the eye socket on an angle and dig out the eyeball.

STEP 5 Make a few shallow incisions around the snout and peel off the thick skin. The snout skin is edible but may be tough. Scrape off the surrounding meat with the fork.

STEP 6 Turn the head upside down. Scoop the meat out of the jaw with the fork, using the knife to cut away any sections stuck to the bone. Pull the jaw away from the rest of the skull, and cut out the tongue. Slice the tongue and eat it.

STEP 7 Look over the rest of the skull and work out any remaining bits of meat.

Use the knife and fork as much as you can to extract the meat, but to get into all the nooks and crannies you will likely have to use your fingers. Keep a napkin nearby and try to minimize mess.

PIG'S HEAD ALERT!

While a traditional pig's head is common in most cultures, it's rare to see a full pig's head on a restaurant menu (if you do, consider yourself lucky and order it immediately). A more common offering is headcheese, a jellied mixture made with bits of meat and gelatin pulled from the pig's head.

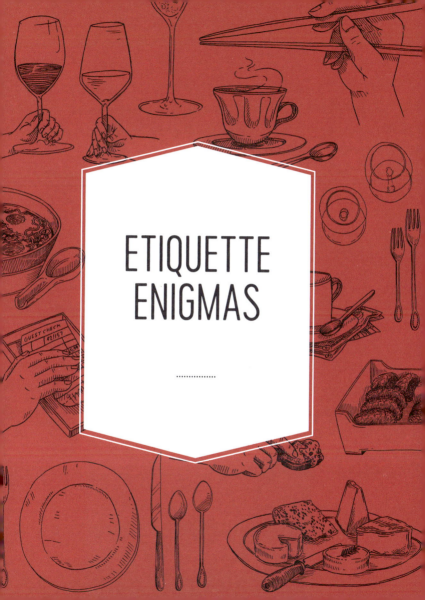

ETIQUETTE ENIGMAS

· · · · · · · · · · · · · · ·

USE THE CORRECT FORK

Navigate a formal table setting with ease.

YOU WILL NEED

Table setting

Table settings are usually arranged according to the courses of a meal, with the utensils to be used first located on the outermost edges. When in doubt, work from the outside in. Here are some dishes you might encounter, depending on the foods being served and how formal the meal is.

Dinner plate: Front and center.

Bread and butter plate: A smaller plate placed above the forks, on the top left of the place setting.

Napkin: Find it on top of or to the left of the dinner plate when you arrive. Lay it across your lap after you sit down so that it's close at hand when you need it.

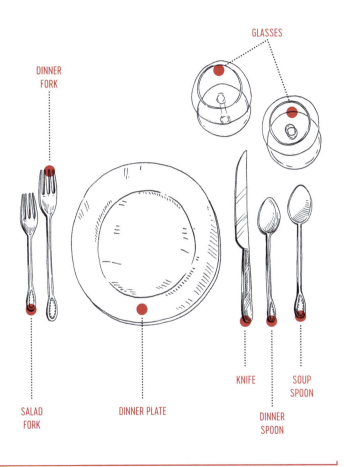

GLASSES

DINNER
FORK

SALAD
FORK

DINNER PLATE

KNIFE

DINNER
SPOON

SOUP
SPOON

Salad fork: This small fork has shorter tines than those on a dinner fork. It is on the far left of the dinner plate.

Fish fork: If a fish course will be served, this fork, which is smaller than a dinner fork and has wider tines, will be located between the salad and dinner forks.

Dinner fork: The dinner fork has longer tines. It is closest to the left side of the dinner plate.

Dessert fork: The dessert fork may be distributed when the dessert course is served or set above the dinner plate, below the dessert spoon, at the start of the meal.

Cocktail fork: Also called a seafood fork or oyster fork, this small, three-tined utensil is used for eating small appetizers, especially seafood. It's placed to the right of the soup spoon, and sometimes the tines are placed in the bowl of the soup spoon with the handle angled off to the right.

Soup spoon: Wider and rounder than a dinner spoon, it is on the far right of the dinner plate.

Dinner spoon: The dinner spoon is narrower than a soup spoon and comes to a gentle point. It is the spoon closest to the dinner plate on the right side.

Dessert spoon: If the dessert spoon isn't passed out with dessert, look for it above the dinner plate directly above the dessert fork.

Butter knife: This small spreader is placed on top of the bread and butter plate, with its handle to the right.

Dinner knife: This is closest to the right side of the plate, with the blade facing the plate.

Fish knife: Find this smaller, wider knife with a flat blade to the right of the dinner knife and to the left of the spoons. It's convenient for lifting pieces to your fork, and it comes in handy if you're eating a whole fish (see page 12).

Salad knife: If your salad requires a knife, this utensil will be placed between the fish knife and the spoons.

Glasses: Both wineglasses and water glasses are placed above the knife and spoons on the top right of the place setting.

Soup bowl: If soup is being served, this bowl will be placed on top of the dinner plate.

> **66** Traditionally, a luncheon is a lunch that takes an eon. **99**
>
> *MISS MANNERS' GUIDE TO EXCRUCIATINGLY CORRECT BEHAVIOR*

USE CHOPSTICKS

With a little practice, you'll never need
to opt for Western utensils.

YOU WILL NEED

Pair of chopsticks

Food to practice on

STEP 1 Place one chopstick in the space between your thumb and forefinger. Rest it on your middle finger to keep it in place.

STEP 2 Hold the second chopstick like a pencil between the tips of your forefinger and thumb. Tap the tips of the chopsticks on the table to make sure they're aligned.

STEP 3 Move only the top chopstick, keeping the other stick stationary. Use the tips of the chopsticks to pick up food. (Note: If you're eating soup with chopsticks, it is acceptable to bring the bowl to your lips and use the chopsticks to guide bits of food from the bowl to your mouth.)

Never cross your chopsticks or stick them upright in your food—both are symbols of death. Also, never rub chopsticks together. Only cheap sticks will splinter, and to assume yours will is in poor taste.

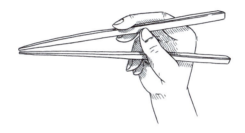

TASTE CHEESE

Whether served as finger foods, light snacks, or a formal course following a meal, cheeses can be surprisingly complex.

YOU WILL NEED

A variety of cheeses on a cheese plate

A cheese knife or small knife

Plain crackers for palate cleansing (optional)

Begin with the softer cheeses that crumble easily off the block or are spreadable; these tend to be mild in flavor. Save harder and sharper cheeses (ones that hold their shape when cut) for the end of your tasting; otherwise, their flavor may overpower anything you taste after them. If the cheese has come straight from the fridge, allow it to warm to room temperature before tasting. Cold can dull cheese's flavor.

Sight is the first way to learn to appreciate and differentiate cheeses. Look at the cheese: What is it cased in? Is it soft or hard? Are there cracks or crystals in the surface? Notice the color and consistency of the rind and the cheese within it, known as the pate.

Next, smell the cheese: Break off a piece with your fingers and bring it to your nose. Take a deep whiff and try to pick up on the flavors. This will help you taste the cheese fully, for smell contributes largely to the experience of tasting.

Finally, put the cheese into your mouth. Chew slowly to release the full flavor, and breathe while you chew. Pay attention; flavors you notice at the beginning of the bite may be different from what you experience at the end. Although you might be tempted to eat the cheese on a cracker, you can fully enjoy the flavor of each cheese if you eat it alone and use crackers as a palate cleanser between tastings.

Cheese Cheat Sheet

Here are some terms you might encounter at a cheese tasting. If you eat enough of the cheese, you'll know this lingo in no time.

TYPE OF CHEESE	DEFINITION	EXAMPLE
Fresh	A cheese that has a lot of moisture. These tend to be creamy and spreadable and have a short shelf life.	Ricotta Chèvre
Soft-ripened	A very soft cheese that has been ripened from the outside in. It's likely to have an edible white rind.	Brie Camembert
Semisoft	A smooth, moist cheese that will likely be creamy and have little or no rind.	Havarti Monterey Jack
Firm/hard	A dense cheese with a consistency ranging from fudgelike to solid. These have less moisture than softer cheeses.	Gouda Cheddar Parmesan
Blue	A cheese with a blue mold growing through the inside.	Gorgonzola Stilton

CHEESE ALERT!

Cheese is an amazing food. It is made by letting milk, usually cow's milk or goat's milk, thicken and separate into solid and liquid parts, which are known as curds and whey. The equation to make cheese is basically dairy solids plus time. There are two major types: fresh cheese and ripened cheese. Fresh cheese is made after the milk separates into curds and whey. Ripened cheese is left to age and develop flavors. Compare a fresh cheese, such as cream cheese or ricotta, to an aged cheese with sharper, nuttier tones, such as gruyère. The longer the cheese ages, the more complex the flavor. Molds are sometimes added for further depth of flavor, such as with pungent blue or creamy brie cheese.

"How can you govern a country which has two hundred and forty-six varieties of cheese?"

CHARLES DE GAULLE

EAT NOODLES

You know that classic scene from *Lady and the Tramp* with the adorable dogs and the spaghetti kiss? Nope, don't do that.

YOU WILL NEED

A prepared noodle dish

Fork

Spoon

STEP 1 Catch a few noodles on the tines of a fork; don't take an entire forkful. Use a spoon to guide the noodles onto the fork.

STEP 2 Twirl the fork against the bowl of the spoon so the noodles wind around the fork in a nest shape.

STEP 3 Bring the fork to your mouth and eat the noodles in one bite.

 If you're eating an Asian noodle dish, use chopsticks to bring the noodles to your mouth. It's acceptable to slurp them up, but don't be noisy.

"It's the sense of what family is at the dinner table. It was the joy of knowing Mother was in the kitchen making our favorite dish. I wish more people would do this and recall the joy of life.**"**

PAUL PRUDHOMME

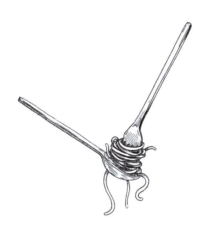

SIP SOUP

If nothing else, remember this: Do. Not. Slurp.

YOU WILL NEED

Crackers (optional)

Bowl of soup

Soup spoon

STEP 1 If you're eating soup with crackers, drop them into the bowl one at a time.

STEP 2 Using your spoon, scoop the soup away from you, toward the center of the table. This prevents drips from falling onto your lap.

STEP 3 Gently bring the spoon to your lips. Sip from the side of the spoon, not the tip.

STEP 4 Do not slurp. We can't emphasize this enough.

STEP 5 Repeat steps 2–4. To get the last bit of liquid from the near-empty bowl, tilt the bowl away from you and use the spoon to scoop up what's left.

STEP 6 When you're finished not slurping, place your spoon on the plate underneath the bowl or in the bowl if there isn't a plate.

TECHNIQUE VARIATIONS

- To eat French onion soup, use the edge of your spoon to cut off bits of the bread and cheese, and eat each spoonful in one full bite.

- If the soup has large pieces of food in it, such as meatballs or matzo balls, gently cut them with a knife or the edge of your spoon before consuming them.

- Asian soups and noodle bowls are served with chopsticks and occasionally a wide spoon. If a spoon is provided, use the chopsticks to place noodles and solids in the bowl of the spoon with a bit of broth, and bring the spoon to your mouth to eat. Otherwise, bring the bowl to your lips to drink the liquid and use the chopsticks to pick out and eat bits of food.

" Good manners: the noise you don't make when you're eating soup. **"**

BENNETT CERF

HOLD A WINEGLASS

How you hold a wineglass is the key to consuming reds and whites at the optimal temperatures. It's also the key to at least looking like you know what you're doing.

YOU WILL NEED

A glass of delicious wine

Your hands

Red Wine: Cup the bowl of the glass in your hand.

White Wine: Hold the glass by the stem, pinched between your index finger and thumb.

Why: Your hands are warm. If you hold the bowl of the glass, the heat from your hand will transfer to the wine and warm it up. Typically, white wine is served cold and red wine is served closer to room temperature, hence the different approaches for holding each type.

TIP To clean a wineglass, cup the bowl of the glass in your hand. Use a stemware brush with foam bristles and a little dish detergent to clean the inside and rim of the glass. Rinse carefully with hot water. Turn the glass upside down and let it air-dry. If you have crystal glasses and they start to develop a film, dilute a little white vinegar in water and soak them in it.

TECHNIQUE VARIATIONS

What do you do when someone hands you a glass of Champagne? What about other glasses?

- Brandy snifter: Hold the glass by the bowl. Your hand's warmth brings out some of the spirit's aromas.

- Champagne flute: Hold the glass by the stem, not the bowl. This allows you to enjoy the bubbly chilled and to see the bubbles moving through the liquid unobstructed by your fingers (or fingerprints).

- Cocktail glass, also known as a martini glass: Hold the glass by the stem. Balance the bottom with your other hand if necessary. Try to find smaller glasses; if your drink is too big, it will get warm before you finish it.

- Stemless glass: If your host serves white wine in a stemless glass, you must consume it as quickly as possible before it warms to room temperature.

❝ Once . . . in the wilds of Afghanistan, I lost my corkscrew, and we were forced to live on nothing but food and water for days. **❞**

W. C. FIELDS, *MY LITTLE CHICKADEE*

HOW TO

TASTE WINE

Resist the urge to down your glass. Instead, show off your wine know-how with these tips.

YOU WILL NEED

Wine

Tasting glass

Glass of water (optional)

Spitting bucket (optional)

Expert sommeliers use these steps to distinguish wine down to the year it was bottled. You can use them to remember what types of wine you like best.

Note: These tips are for wine tastings at which you'll be trying multiple bottles, but the same rules apply when you're tasting a bottle you've purchased at a restaurant. The person who ordered the wine follows these steps to confirm that it's up to par before sharing it with the table.

See: Look at the wine in the glass. What color is it? Deep red? Light pink? Is it transparent?

Swirl: Gently swirl the wine and notice how the liquid slides along the inside of the glass. Full-bodied wines, which often have bold flavors, are more viscous and will slide more slowly around the glass. Lighter wines are thinner and will slide quickly around the glass; they have a less powerful but still pleasant taste. Swirling also aerates the wine, releasing the aromatics and the full flavor.

Smell: Now that those aromas are swirling, stick your nose into the glass and take a deep breath. Try to pick out the different aromas. Fruit, oak, caramel, vanilla . . . try to discern the flavors before you taste the wine.

Sip: Resist the urge to gulp and instead take a small sip. Move the wine around in your mouth and let it settle on your tongue. See if you detect any of the flavors you smelled in the glass.

Savor: Now you want to mix some air with the wine in your mouth, so that the flavors become even more apparent. Take a small breath through your lips and move the wine around as you do so—like a little kid blowing bubbles, but backward. This may look funny.

Spit (optional): If you will be sampling more than one wine, you may want to spit the wine into the bucket provided after tasting, to ensure that you keep a clear head throughout the experience.

TIP If water is served, rinse your wineglass and take a small sip before the next tasting so that the different wines' flavors don't mix in the glass or your mouth. If water isn't provided, take a tiny sip of your next wine before fully tasting it to eliminate flavors lingering in your mouth from the previous pour.

> **" Wine is the most healthful and most hygienic of beverages. "**
>
> LOUIS PASTEUR

HOW TO

MAKE A TOAST

You want people to pull out their phones and record your speech because it's memorable, not because you had too many cocktails beforehand . . .

YOU WILL NEED

A room full of people

Glass of champagne, wine, or another drink

Butter knife

STEP 1 Decide what you're going to say in advance. Keep it short. Write it down and practice it. You may feel silly rehearsing, but doing so helps you know how long the speech will be and helps you memorize it. Keep your audience in mind while you write. For example, avoid off-color jokes in polite company or in groups of people whom you don't know well.

STEP 2 Know when you're on. If someone else is hosting, that person makes the first toast. If you're the first toaster, wait for a lull in activity. You don't want to compete with a full dance floor or dinner service. After most of the room has nearly finished eating is a good time.

STEP 3 Stand at your seat and gently tap your glass with a butter knife to get the attention of the room.

STEP 4 Give your toast. If you're not a seasoned public speaker, the spotlight can be intimidating. Follow these tips for a smooth and memorable speech:

- Position your feet a little farther than shoulder width apart. You might feel weird standing like this, but you won't look weird, and your stance will keep you from swaying or shifting your weight back and forth. In other words, your audience won't get seasick watching you.

- Bend your knees slightly. Locking them increases your chances of fainting.

- Hold your drink in one hand. Hold your notes or a microphone in the other, or rest your free hand gently on the table or at your side.

- Speak loudly, confidently, and more slowly than you think you should. If you're nervous, you're almost certainly talking faster than you realize.

- Make eye contact. Look around the room and connect with people, not your feet or your notes. You memorized this, remember?

- Don't apologize or make a disclaimer like "I'm not much of a speaker, but . . ." Just let people enjoy your toast. When they tell you later that they loved it, simply say thank you.

- Still have stage fright? Take a deep breath and think about why you're giving the toast. Whether it's for a cause you believe in or your best friend getting married, you agreed to this for a good reason. Let it motivate you. If all else fails, look at the clock. In an hour your speech will be long over and you'll be enjoying that champagne and dancing the night away.

STEP 5 End with your glass raised high, and then take a sip.

 The event and your role in it will dictate the length of your speech. As the best man or maid of honor at a wedding, for example, you can speak for a bit longer than if you're simply toasting a relative's nuptials.

— TOASTING ALERT! —

Some people consider it bad luck to toast with water. Still, toasting with water is more polite than sitting it out. If you're the recipient of the toast (congrats!), stand and acknowledge it gracefully, but don't drink to yourself.

DRINK TEA

You don't have to point your pinkie, we promise.

YOU WILL NEED

- Tea
- Teacup and saucer
- Teaspoon
- Milk (optional)
- Sugar (optional)

STEP 1 At a formal tea gathering, the host will pour your tea. If you are served hot water and tea bags or loose leaves in a tea strainer, place the tea in the water and steep for 3 to 5 minutes.

STEP 2 Remove tea bag or strainer. Stir in milk and sugar (if desired). Do not let the teaspoon hit the edges of the teacup; this is considered impolite. When you're done stirring, place the teaspoon on the saucer.

STEP 3 Hold your teacup with one hand, curling your index finger around the handle and placing your thumb on top of the handle. Rest your middle finger under the bottom curve of the handle, and curl your ring finger and pinkie into your palm.

STEP 4 Look down into your teacup as you sip so you don't spill tea on yourself.

 TIP If the teacups are antiques, you may want to pour the milk in first so the sudden heat of the tea does not crack the cup.

— TEA ALERT! —

Each culture approaches tea in a different way. These rules apply to a traditional English-style tea party or afternoon tea—a light meal between lunch and dinner where tea is served. If you're unsure what customs are appropriate to a tea situation, look to your host, who will typically lead the service and offer etiquette clues. Also pay attention to other guests, who may be more familiar with the style of tea service.

USE BREAD AS A UTENSIL

In some cultures, bread is the only utensil at the table. In Ethiopian cuisine, for example, meals are consumed with pieces of *injera*, a spongy flatbread. Here's the lowdown on substituting silverware with your favorite carbs.

YOU WILL NEED

Bread

Soup or sauce-based meal

STEP 1 Tear off a bite-sized piece of bread—do not use the whole roll or slice, since that would require double dipping, an etiquette no-no—and hold one end with your fingertips.

STEP 2 Scoop the sauce into the bread by pushing it away from you, to ensure that drips fall back onto the plate and not onto you. Take care not to get sauce on your hands.

STEP 3 Eat the piece of bread in one bite.

> **❝The art of bread making can become a consuming hobby, and no matter how often and how many kinds of bread one has made, there always seems to be something new to learn.❞**
>
> JULIA CHILD

EAT SUSHI

In Japan, eating sushi is a practice with an entire set of customs and traditions. What follows are the most important tips for eating in Western sushi joints.

YOU WILL NEED

Sushi

Chopsticks

Soy sauce (optional)

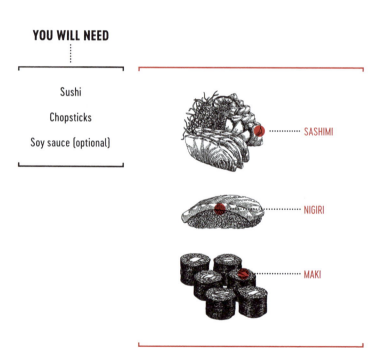

SASHIMI

NIGIRI

MAKI

STEP 1 Before ordering, familiarize yourself with the different types of sushi.

- Sashimi: Though the word literally means "sliced meat" in Japanese, at most sushi restaurants it refers to slices of raw (or occasionally boiled) fish. These slices are not served with sushi rice.

- Nigiri: This refers to a hand-pressed rectangle of sushi rice with a topping like cooked or raw seafood or omelet.

- Maki: Fish, vegetables, rice, and other ingredients that are rolled with nori (seaweed) or soy paper and sliced are known as maki.

STEP 2 Place your order. Don't ask if the fish is fresh; it's insulting. Instead, if you don't know what to select, ask the chef for suggestions. You may end up with something that hasn't even made it to the menu yet.

STEP 3 Use chopsticks to pick up sashimi pieces. Nigiri and maki may be eaten with chopsticks or your fingers.

STEP 4 If you'd like to dip a piece in the provided soy or ponzu sauce, do so gingerly so as not to saturate the sushi. Wasabi should not be mixed into the soy sauce; place a little bit directly on the food.

STEP 5 Place the entire piece in your mouth and chew slowly, savoring the fish. If a piece of sushi is too large to eat in one bite, do not put it back on your plate. Take a bite, hold it with your chopsticks or fingers until you finish chewing, and then immediately eat the rest.

STEP 6 Eat the provided pickled ginger between sushi servings to cleanse your palate.

STEP 7 If you're sharing sushi with others, turn your chopsticks around before picking up a piece from someone else's plate so that you don't touch the food with the end that has been in your mouth. Place it on your plate and then turn the chopsticks back to the original position before eating.

STEP 8 If you're sitting at the bar, don't hand money to the chef. Sushi chefs take cleanliness very seriously and will not touch the money.

TIP

In most of the United States, the minimum wage for people who earn tips is between $2 and $3 per hour, and much of that goes to taxes before your server ever sees it. A general guideline is to tip your server 15% to 20% of the total bill.

At a Restaurant

Less than 15%: Not recommended unless service was unacceptable.

15%: Adequate service.

18%: Good service. The server was acceptable and your party is pleased.

20%: Great service. The server gave your party everything you needed in a timely manner. You have no complaints.

More than 20%: Excellent service. The server went above and beyond the required duties.

At a Bar

Typically you should tip a bartender 20% of the total tab, or more if service was exceptional. However, don't tip below $1 per beer or wine, or $2 per cocktail, and leave more if the drinks are complicated to make or the bar was busy.

At a Coffee Shop

Counter service employees are paid a full hourly wage, but if you spot a tip jar at the register, leaving a small tip is welcome—especially if you have a complicated order. A dollar per beverage or item is typical.

Delivery and Take-Out

These workers also receive hourly wages, but a 10% to 15% tip is appropriate if your order has been prepared correctly and delivered to you hot.

 It's much faster to calculate a 20% tip in your head than it is to pull out your phone. Look at the total amount of your bill. Move the decimal one place to the left. You remember this from school—that's 10%. Now multiply by 2 to get your tip.

— TIPPING ALERT! —

Tipping is commonplace in America, but in other places a tip of 10% or less, if anything, is typical. In fact, in many Asian countries tipping is considered rude except for service at a luxury hotel or restaurant. Before you travel to a new country, research the local customs so you don't commit a tipping faux pas.

DECIDE WHO PAYS THE BILL

Learn how to divvy up checks the modern way.

YOU WILL NEED

A dinner date

Bill at the end of the meal

Money

Gone are the days when the gentleman was expected to pay for the lady. Nowadays, the general rule is if you initiated the plans, you will be paying, or at least paying your own share. The rule applies both to one-on-one dates as well as groups, such as if you invite your partner's parents to join the two of you for a meal.

If you are the invitee, however, you should always offer to pay for your share, unless it has been explicitly stated that you are being treated. Some people will insist on paying for the entire bill. Thank them for their generosity, and offer to pick up the tab next time.

If the costs of your party's meals are fairly similar, it's often easier to split the bill evenly.

However, if there are a variety of costs and items among members of the party, and if only a few folks ordered drinks or dessert, you may decide to divide the bill individually. If you split the bill and want to pay with credit cards, find out if the restaurant will let you pay with multiple cards. Some have restrictions on the number of ways you can pay.

 TIP If you're in a business meeting, typically the person who set up the meeting will pay. If you're the client, you'll likely be taken care of.

ORDER FROM THE MENU

You have questions. Fortunately, your server has answers.

YOU WILL NEED

Menu

Your server

Curiosity

In any restaurant worth its salt, the servers will be knowledgeable about everything on the menu, including ingredients and preparation. A good rule of thumb is to order what the restaurant is known for or whatever the chef's recommendations are. If you still can't choose, simply ask, "What would you suggest?" or "What do you order here?" A good server will be happy to note popular items and personal favorites. Some may also be able to request adjustments to suit your needs. Just keep requests within reason and remember how helpful the server was come tipping time.

Most restaurants have a website or social media presence, so it's easy to look up the menu before you visit. It may not include daily specials but will give you an idea of what to expect, including price ranges and offerings for special diets. Also worth noting: It may or may not be true, but supposedly diners look at the top right-hand corner of the menu first. You're likely to find the most expensive dishes there. These may be surrounded by items that bring the restaurant a high profit margin. If you're on a budget, read the entire menu before choosing your meal.

Before your first visit, check online reviews, but take them with a grain of salt. Often people will post about either excellent or terrible experiences, but nothing in between.

Trying to eat healthfully? The menu likely won't include nutritional information, but here are some guidelines to keep in mind:

- Decide what to order before becoming very hungry or having a drink.

- Start with a clear soup or a salad. Ask for dressing on the side.

- Skip the bread. Save room for vegetables!

- Try to swap out fries for a side of vegetables or salad. It's not always possible, but it's worth asking.

- Avoid fried foods. Opt for baked seafood or leaner cuts of meat.

- Restaurant portions are often much larger than what you'd serve yourself at home. Before you take a bite, ask for a to-go box and wrap up one-third to one-half of your meal. Then set it aside and take it home for lunch or dinner the next day.

Feeling adventurous? Politely ask the server if you may order off menu. If so, request the chef's favorite meal to make. This is especially fun in sushi restaurants.

TIP Beware of the "specials" at chain restaurants. If the server offers off-menu items that are not listed in an insert and does not mention they're doing a menu preview, it's likely that the kitchen is trying to get rid of ingredients that are about to go bad.

— DATE ALERT! —

Occasionally you may find yourself having a meal with someone you don't know well and wanting to make a good impression. Maybe it's a job interview, a date, a potential client, or your favorite celebrity. Don't panic.

- First and foremost, order what you'd like to eat. Women don't have to be restricted to salad on a first date, and men do not need to assert their manliness by ordering a steak. And nobody needs to act like a pretentious foodie to be impressive.

- Avoid messy foods. You probably spent an hour fretting over the perfect outfit; don't risk dribbling down your front!

- Keep alcohol consumption to a minimum. You might be nervous, but try to take a few deep breaths instead of a few quick shots.

- If you'll be doing a lot of close talking, avoid garlic, onions, or other foods with a strong smell.

- Keep a few breath mints handy, just in case.

- If you think you'll be nervous, arrive a little early and try to relax. Sit in your car, outside on a bench, or even at the restaurant's bar. (No need to start drinking, of course. A tonic and lime is a beautiful thing.) On a practical level, you won't arrive late or rushed due to unexpected traffic or a wrong turn. And giving yourself a few minutes to gather your thoughts can make you feel much more comfortable.

- Try to get to know the other person, who may be just as nervous as you. Fortunately, food is a great conversation starter. With any luck, you'll be enjoying the conversation before long. Have fun!

EXCUSE YOURSELF FROM THE TABLE

Ghosting is not appropriate in polite company.

YOU WILL NEED

Dinner companions

Napkin

Subtlety

STEP 1 To step away from the table temporarily, wait for a pause in conversation; don't interrupt someone. Say "excuse me" or "I'll be right back." Don't explain that you are going to the restroom, to take a call, or whatever else you plan to do.

STEP 2 Loosely fold your napkin and leave it to the left of your plate or on your seat—don't crumple it. At a restaurant, you may be given a fresh napkin upon your return.

STEP 3 The host placing her napkin on the table is the cue that dinner is over. You may now do the same. Thank your host and say goodbye to the rest of the guests.

TIP If you're leaving dinner for good, do so when coffee is served, after dessert has ended.

66 The shared meal elevates eating from a mechanical process of fueling the body to a ritual of family and community, from the mere animal biology to an act of culture. **99**

MICHAEL POLLAN

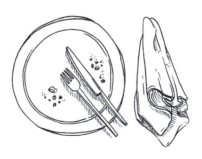

FOODIE
FIXES

·············

EAT SOMETHING SPICY

Can't handle the heat? These tips will save you some pain.

YOU WILL NEED

Spicy food

Glass of ice water

Starchy side dish such as bread, crackers, or potatoes

Glass of milk

STEP 1 Before taking your first bite, drink a full mouthful of ice water. The ice water will numb your mouth, making it easier to consume something potentially painful. (Note: Don't drink ice water *after* eating spicy food; it will spread the heat around your mouth and only worsen the sting.)

STEP 2 Start slow. If possible, first try something slightly above your current tolerance, such as medium salsa rather than mild. Don't attempt the triple-habanero variety right off the bat, especially if you're not used to spicy foods.

STEP 3 Take slow, deliberate bites and chew well. Eating quickly will give you less control over the burn.

STEP 4   Alternate your tastes with bites of a starchy side dish, which will help absorb the heat.

STEP 5   After you finish eating, drink a glass of milk. Dairy products contain a protein that helps soothe your mouth and temper the spice.

SPICE ALERT!

Multiple theories explain why people seek out and brag about eating foods that cause pain. Perhaps we like chilies because they offer health benefits, like lower blood pressure. Or maybe, as professor of psychology Dr. Paul Rozin suggests, it's possible that we tend to enjoy some "benign masochism" with our hot sauce.

Scoville Ratings

If you have trouble with spicy food, avoid anything that advertises a Scoville rating. Named after its creator, Wilbur Scoville, the scale measures the concentration of capsaicin, the substance that makes peppers spicy. A bell pepper is rated 0 Scoville heat units (SHU), and cayenne pepper generally earns between 30,000 and 50,000 SHU.

Due to genetic cross-breeding and newly discovered species, the World's Hottest Pepper changes every few years. As of 2016, the reigning champion is the Carolina Reaper, which clocks in at 2.2 million SHU.

SHU OF COMMON PEPPERS	
Habanero	350,000
Thai	100,000
Cayenne	50,000
Serrano	23,000
Chipotle	8,000
Jalapeño	8,000
Poblano	1,500
Banana	500
Bell Pepper	0

EAT SOMETHING MESSY

Enjoying a sloppy joe doesn't mean you have to be a sloppy you.

YOU WILL NEED

Messy food

Fork

Knife

Napkin

Moist towelette

STEP 1   Have your napkin at the ready to wipe up spills, whether they're on your face or down your front. Messy foods can be unpredictable.

STEP 2   Use a knife and fork whenever possible. They might not make a difference with overstuffed sandwiches or greasy chicken wings, but you can use them to pull the meat off a BBQ rib without getting sauce under your fingernails.

STEP 3   If the food must be consumed with your hands, use both of them to hold it. Lean over your plate so that drips land there instead of in your lap.

STEP 4   Take small bites. This gives you better control over what you're eating.

STEP 5   Use a fork, not your hands, to eat bits of food that have fallen onto your plate.

STEP 6   After eating, use the moist towelette to clean your hands and face, if needed.

“**Barbecue may not be the road to world peace, but it's a start.**”

ANTHONY BOURDAIN

PACE YOURSELF WHEN DRINKING

Enjoy a night out, but stay in control. Bonus: some of these tips may help prevent a hangover, too!

- Never drink liquour on an empty stomach. Having a heavy, fatty meal beforehand will slow your body's absorption of alcohol.

- Limit consumption to one drink an hour, at most.

- Drink with friends, and don't stay glued to your phone the whole time. The more you talk and socialize, the less time you'll have to gulp down your drink.

- Stick to beer and wine, which contain less alcohol than mixed drinks and are unaffected by the generous pours of a heavy-handed bartender.

- Alternate cups of water with cups of booze to stay hydrated, help pace your liquor consumption, and prevent a hangover.

- Just say no to shots. They're a surefire way to let a buzz get away from you.

- Pick a drink and stick to it. Although the old saying "Beer before liquor, never been sicker; liquor before beer, you're in the clear" isn't exactly truthful, you'll have a harder time keeping track of your intake when drinking a variety of cocktails or spirits of different alcohol contents.

- Want to make a glass of wine last longer? Pour in a bit of lime soda or sparkling water. Instant spritzer!

- **Obvious Warning:** Don't drink to excess, and never drive drunk, even if you feel okay to drive. Alcohol can take a long time to metabolize and you may think you're soberer than you are. There are plenty of phone apps that will get you a safe ride home. Use them.

> **"A vine bears three grapes, the first of pleasure, the second of drunkenness, and the third of repentance."**
>
> ANACHARSIS

STAY VEGETARIAN AT A BARBECUE

Because sometimes you must socialize with carnivores.

- Bring a dish to share withs. Doing so will ensure a vegetarian option, and—bonus—you can show the meat eaters that veggie-centric dishes are delicious.

- BYO burger—after clearing it with the host—to cook for yourself. With food allergies and special diets becoming more common, it's no longer out of the ordinary to see someone eating their own meal at a social gathering.

- Load your plate with side dishes. Even when the main event is a slab of meat, you're likely to find a variety of sides that are vegetarian. Cole slaw, potato salad, and crudités are all safe bets. Be careful about green beans that may be cooked with bacon or saucy sides that may include an animal stock.

- Are the hosts close friends of yours? Call them ahead of time and ask what they plan to serve. They may be willing to pick up veggie burgers or another meatless item for you. They might even modify some of their side dishes—by omitting bacon, using vegetable stock instead of chicken stock, etc.

- If all else fails, or if you're truly worried you won't have any options, eat a full meal before the barbecue.

VEGETARIAN ALERT!

Are you hosting a vegetarian or vegan friend at your barbecue? While you cook, keep track of dishes that contain animal products. Read ingredients lists carefully, and watch out for these surprises:

- Red food dye: Natural red #4, cochineal, carminic acid, or carmine, which is found in pasta sauce and other red foods, is made from beetles.

- Orange juice: Fortified varieties often contain fish oil or lanolin, which is made from wool. Look for OJ without added omega-3s, or squeeze your own.

- White sugar: Refined white sugar is processed with cattle bones.

- Gelatin: Because it is made from animal products like bones and hooves, gelatin is a no-no for vegans. Unfortunately, that rules out the Jell-O salad, a lot of candies, some yogurts, and marshmallows.

- Anchovies: These tiny fish turn up in some surprising places, like Caesar salad dressing and Worcestershire sauce.

- Lard: Cake mixes, pie crusts, refried beans, and tortillas may contain lard.

- Beer and wine: Some drinks are clarified with fish bladders, and others are vegetarian.

- Cheese: Rennet, which is made from sheep stomachs, is an ingredient in some cheeses.

66 Nothing will benefit human health and increase the chances for survival of life on earth as much as the evolution to a vegetarian diet. **99**

ALBERT EINSTEIN

STICK TO YOUR DIET AT A PARTY

It's week 3 of your diet, arguably the roughest stretch
to get through, and suddenly you find yourself face-to-face
with a festive buffet at a wedding, baby shower, or happy hour.
Here's how to stay on the wagon.

- Eat before the party so that you're full of diet-friendly food and less likely to fill your plate with calorie-laden hors d'oeuvres.

- If you're hungry, choose wisely—party staples like fresh fruit, veggie crudités, cheeses, and baked chips and salsa won't kill your diet. Try to make the same choices you would make at home: grilled chicken instead of a bacon-covered burger, vegetables instead of potato chips, fruit instead of cupcakes, and the like.

- Grab a smaller plate, and don't go back for seconds. Setting limits is a helpful way to ensure you stick to your diet. Studies show that smaller plates make it easier to stop when you're full.

- Alcohol is the downfall of many a diet, so try to avoid it. If you can't help but have an alcoholic beverage, opt for clear liquors with no-sugar mixers, like a vodka soda with a squeeze of lime. Choose a mixed drink that's easy to dilute if you want the same amount of liquor to last longer, and alternate alcoholic drinks with glasses of water.

- Don't feel the need to explain. Peer pressure can be intense when people notice you're not taking advantage of the spread. But nobody should have a say in your food choices except you (and in some cases, your doctor). A diet is a personal decision. If someone inquires why you're not partaking in the triple-stuffed, double-stacked potato skins, feel free to simply smile and shrug.

- If the hosts are close friends of yours, casually mention ahead of time that you're cutting down on sugar (or whatever your personal dieting tactic is). They'll more than likely be supportive—after all, they're your friends. Maybe that means they'll prepare more vegetable sides or serve fruit with dessert. Maybe it just means they won't shove the cupcakes in your face. Either way, why not have them on your side?

- Be positive. You may be tempted to think—or worse, say—things like "Do you know how many calories are in that dip?!" or "Too bad I can't have those cookies." Instead, focus on how delicious the fresh fruit salad is or how amazing your host's homegrown tomatoes taste. You'll be happier, and your host will get some well-deserved praise.

- Have a good time. What else is going on at this party other than food? Play darts. Look through photos. Get in the pool. Ask for a tour of the backyard. Play with the kids. Get into a conversation with someone you don't know—not about food. You won't have time to dwell on the fried cheese appetizers.

- Keep the big picture in mind. You started your diet before you got to this party, and you're a smart decision maker. Remind yourself of your goal when you're tempted to blow it.

"My doctor told me to stop having intimate dinners for four. Unless there are three other people."

ORSON WELLES

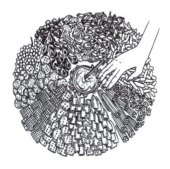

FIX BAD BREATH

The alternative is to breathe through your nose and avoid speaking.

- Take preventative measures. The easiest way to fix bad breath is to prevent it from happening. Don't smoke. Brush your teeth twice a day (don't forget to scrape your tongue!) and gargle with mouthwash. Avoid foods like onion and garlic and drinks like coffee, whose odor will linger on your breath. If a food has a sharp smell, it's likely that smell will occupy your mouth, too.

- Chew sugarless gum. The sugar in mints and regular gum will feed the bacteria in your mouth, making bad breath even worse.

- Drink water. Saliva can help prevent bad breath, and water will encourage saliva production.

- Rinse stinky food particles out of your mouth with plain water or soda water.

- Is there a sprig of parsley on your plate? Mint leaves in your mojito? Chew on green herbs like these to counter bad breath with a strong but pleasant scent. Just don't grab chives; their oniony odor won't do you any favors.

- Nibble some nuts or another hard, abrasive snack. The texture will help loosen food particles that may be causing an odor in your mouth.

 Not sure if you have bad breath? Sneak off to the bathroom and floss. If the floss smells bad, your breath probably does as well.

HANDLE BEANS

Beans, beans, the musical fruit . . . you know the rest. Here's how to avoid potentially embarrassing bodily reactions to beans or other foods that disagree with you.

- Identify and avoid your troublesome foods. Some people have issues with beans, fibrous vegetables, or dairy products.

- If the offending food is one you enjoy, you may want to try to build a tolerance to it. Gradually add it to your diet, starting with small portions.

- Stash anti-gas medicine in your wallet or purse if you can't or don't want to avoid the food, and take some before you eat it.

- Ginger has been said to help calm the digestive tract. Grab a ginger beer or ginger candies if you start to feel symptoms of gas or indigestion. Mint, honey, and cinnamon may also help.

- Drink water, which will flush out your digestive tract and help alleviate the gas.

TASTE SOMETHING YOU HATE

Someone lovingly made you a dish . . . try not to squirm.

- Ask for a small portion. Less on your plate means less you have to choke down.

- Take a deep breath. Unless you're allergic, this food isn't going to kill you.

- Take small bites. If your gag reflex is activated, you won't want a mouthful of food.

- Eat with other food or drink. Follow a bite of the offending dish with something more pleasant. If the texture is your concern, take a bite of something with a different texture to mask it. Take a drink to rinse away the flavor.

- Hold your nose, if possible. Smell is a large part of taste, so by blocking your nose you'll diminish the flavor.

- Tell the truth. We're all adults, right? Everyone has likes and dislikes. Feel free to gently inform your host that you don't really care for broccoli.

" Sharing food with another human being
is an intimate act that should not be
indulged in lightly. **"**

M. F. K. FISHER

RECOVER FROM A TONGUE BURN

We've all been there: you're super hungry, or you misjudge how hot the soup is, and suddenly your impatience results in a tongue burn. The good news—the sensation is temporary. Try these cooling tricks.

- Assess the damage. If you've severely burnt your tongue—for example, if it blisters, turns black, or is numb or seriously painful—seek medical attention. You don't want it to become infected. When in doubt, go to a doctor. If the burn is mild, read on.

- Rinse your mouth with cool water, which will temper the heat and wash away food particles that may be clinging to your tongue.

- Drink some milk. It will coat your tongue and relieve the burning sensation.

- Take an anti-inflammatory painkiller like ibuprofen, which will lessen the pain and inflammation.

- Gargle with salt water multiple times a day to promote healing.

- Swish with milk of magnesia to promote cell regrowth. Topical anesthetics can help numb the pain while your tongue heals.

- During healing, avoid eating acidic or abrasive foods, which can irritate the sores.

 Be careful with microwaves! Sometimes they heat food unevenly, so your next bite could be hotter than you expect.

BURN ALERT!

Burning mouth syndrome, also called glossodynia, is the sensation of burning in your mouth that has no apparent reason. It's a chronic pain unrelated to the hot meal you're having.

SEND FOOD BACK

Sometimes something just goes wrong. When that something is your meal, don't be afraid to send it back. Be polite, understand that mistakes happen, and you'll be enjoying your meal in no time.

STEP 1 Take preventative measures: Do you have a food allergy? Or does the thought of an errant mushroom make you gag? Tell your server before ordering. If your allergy is life threatening, call ahead and make sure that the restaurant can accommodate you. Keep in mind that although some kitchens can make changes to dishes, there may be a variety of reasons why your filet mignon simply cannot be divorced from its mushroom sauce.

STEP 2 Inspect your plate and take a maximum of three bites. If something is wrong with the dish (overcooked, undercooked, not as ordered) it is acceptable to request a redo. If the issue is a matter of taste (you took a chance on the salmon even though you're not a huge fan of fish), the server may or may not offer you something else.

STEP 3 Gently request the attention of your server and explain the error. Keep in mind that your server may not be at fault.

STEP 4 At this point, a number of things may happen:

- Your server will take the dish back to the kitchen to be fixed.

- Your server will have the kitchen remake the dish entirely.

- You will be offered a substitute dish.

- If your meal can't be fixed sufficiently and an adequate substitute can't be made, you will not be charged for it.

STEP 5 Once your new plate arrives, inspect it and take a bite. Has the issue been fixed? If so, great. Enjoy! If not, politely (but this time, perhaps more firmly) inform your server. A manager may stop by the table to discuss the issue with you.

STEP 6 Remember to be polite and understanding. And unless you know definitively that the server is wholly at fault, don't let the tip suffer. If you are not charged for your meal, remember to tip the server based on what the total bill would have been had the complimentary portion been included.

STOP YOURSELF FROM CHOKING

Hopefully you'll never need this essential information.

STEP 1 Be prepared. Take a class on CPR and the Heimlich maneuver. Watch videos and study techniques. Whether you're a lifeguard or a data analyst, such lifesaving training is useful—you never know what might happen or where. If you spend a lot of time with kids, consider getting additional child-focused training, which differs from techniques appropriate for adults.

STEP 2 Try to stay calm. It's easy to panic when your airway is suddenly blocked, but you'll be better able to save yourself if you keep a level head.

STEP 3 Try to cough. If you can, it's a sign that air is still getting through. You may be able to dislodge the object this way.

STEP 4 Get the attention of someone nearby, if possible. If you can't speak or make noise, use whatever is at your disposal to draw attention to yourself. Crossing your hands over your throat is the universal sign for "I'm choking."

STEP 5   If no one is around, perform the Heimlich maneuver on yourself. According to the Mayo Clinic: "Call 911 or your local emergency number immediately. Then perform abdominal thrusts to dislodge the item. Place a fist slightly above your navel. Grasp your fist with the other hand and bend over a hard surface—a countertop or chair will do. Shove your fist inward and upward."

STEP 6   Continue until the object is dislodged or medical help arrives.

CPR ALERT!

Look for lifesaving classes at your local hospital, community college, or American Red Cross center (redcross.org). Or search online by location for an American Heart Association–approved course (heart.org). Such classes usually last only a couple of hours and are inexpensive. Whatever price you pay will be worth it should you ever need to use these skills.

❝Be prepared.❞

OFFICIAL SCOUT MOTTO

RESOLVES

These books, websites, and apps will help you further research all your adulting needs.

HOW TO BEHAVE

The Art of Manliness: Classic Skills and Manners for the Modern Man
Brett McKay and Kate McKay

*Good Manners for Nice People Who Sometimes Say F*ck*
Amy Alkon

How to Be a Perfect Stranger: The Essential Religious Etiquette Handbook
Stuart M. Matlins and Arthur J. Magida

I Like You: Hospitality under the Influence
Amy Sedaris

Miss Manners' Guide to Excruciatingly Correct Behavior
Judith Martin and Gloria Kamen

Modern Manners: Tools to Take You to the Top
Dorothea Johnson

Modern Romance
Aziz Ansari

Stuff Every Graduate Should Know
Alyssa Favreau

The Worst Case Scenario Survival Handbook
David Borgenicht and Joshua Piven

HOW TO EAT

The America's Test Kitchen Cooking School Cookbook
America's Test Kitchen

How to Cook Everything: The Basics
Mark Bittman

BeerAdvocate.com

Beer profiles, ratings, and reviews.

Eater.com

National and city-specific guides to restaurants and food news.

Fooducate App (iOS, Android)

Scan a barcode at the grocery store for nutritional value and recommended alternatives.

OpenTable.com

Browse restaurants and make reservations.

Humane Eating Project App (iOS, Android)

Find vegetarian-friendly restaurants and restaurants with humane meat options.

Mixology App (iOS, Android)

Enter your ingredients and discover thousands of cocktail recipes.

Vivino App (iOS, Android, Windows)

Snap a shot of a wine bottle and get reviews and prices.

WineGlass App (iOS)

Snap a shot of the wine list and get ratings and pairing info.

ABOUT THE AUTHOR

Ashley Blom is a Millennial foodie from Hatfield, Massachusetts. She has been writing ever since she could hold a pen or sit at a computer. She currently resides in Austin, Texas, with her fiancé, a rescue dog, and two cats. She enjoys eating (and cooking!) her way through her adopted hometown and writes about it at ForkingUp.com.

ABOUT THE ILLUSTRATOR

Lucy Engelman is an illustrator in the most traditional sense of the word. Her intricate line work often nods to her fascination with the natural world. She has a BFA from the University of Michigan and has worked with *Bon Appétit*, West Elm, Patagonia, and *Runner's World*. Her work has been recognized by the Society for Publication Designers and has been featured on a variety of platforms. She is also staff illustrator for *Collective Quarterly*. Lucy puts pen to paper surrounded by her growing collection of house plants in Pittsburgh, Pennsylvania.

INDEX

A

allergy, food, 146

almonds, 60, 65

animal products in foods, 133

arils, 54

artichoke, 32

Asian soups and noodle dishes, 90, 93

asparagus, 30

avocado, 34, 42

B

bad breath, 138

banana pepper, 126

bananas, 42

beans, 140. *See also* edamame

bell pepper, 126

benign masochism theory of spicy food, 125

berries, 42

bill, how to pay, 114

blue cheese, 88, 89

bowl, soup, 83

Brandy snifter, 96

Brazil nuts, 60, 62, 65

bread as utensil, 106

bread and butter plate, 80

brie cheese, 88

bugs, 28

burned tongue, 144

burning mouth syndrome, 145

butter knife, 83

C

camembert cheese, 88

Carolina Reaper pepper, 126

cashews, 62, 65

cayenne pepper, 126

Champagne flute, 96

check, *see* bill, how to pay

cheddar cheese, 88

cheese, 86–89

chestnuts, 62, 65

chèvre cheese, 88

chicken, 68; homemade stock, 70

chipotle pepper, 126

choking, 148

chopsticks, 84, 90, 93

citrus, 58

cocktail fork, 82

cocktail glass, 96

coconut, 38

corked wine, 100

CPR, 148

crawfish, 21

cream cheese, 89

cricket flour, 28

D

date, 119

dessert fork, 82

dessert spoon, 82

diet, 135

dinner fork, 82

dinner knife, 83

dinner plate, 80

dinner spoon, 82

drinking, 129

durian, 66

E

edamame, 44

entomophagy, 29

escargots, 26

excuse yourself from the table, 120

F

filberts, 62

fish, whole, 12

fish fork, 82

fish knife, 83

flatulence, 140

food allergy, 146

food you hate, how to eat, 142

forks, types of, 82

French onion soup, 93

fruit, how to pick ripe, 42

G

game hens, 72

glasses, 83, 86. *See also* wineglass

glossodynia, 145

gorgonzola cheese, 88

gouda cheese, 88

gruyère cheese, 89

H

habanero pepper, 126

havarti cheese, 88

hazelnuts, 62, 65

headcheese, 77

Heimlich maneuver, 148

I

injera, 106

insects, *see* bugs

J

jalapeño pepper, 126

K

"king of the fruits," 66

knives, types of, 83

kohlrabi, 46

kumquats, 58

L

legumes, *see* beans, edamame,
    peanuts

limequat, 59

lobster, 16

M

macadamia nuts, 62, 65

maki, 108–9

mango, 42, 48

martini glass, 96

matzo ball soup, 93

meatball soup, 93

menu, how to order from, 116

messy food, 127

mocktails, 131

Monterey Jack cheese, 88

mudbugs, 21

N

napkin, 80

nigiri, 108–9

noodles, 90, 93

Nutella, 62

nuts, 60–65

O

order from the menu, 116

oysters, 24

P

papaya, 51

Parmesan cheese, 88

paying the bill, 114

peanuts, 62–63, 65

pecans, 63, 65

pigs' feet, 73

pig's head, 75

pistachios, 63, 65

place setting, *see* table setting

plantains, 42

plates, types of, 80

poblano pepper, 126

pomegranate, 53

poultry, *see* chicken, quail

Q

quail, 71

R

rambutan, 55

raw oysters, 24

ricotta cheese, 88

S

salad fork, 82

salad knife, 83

sashimi, 108–9

Scoville rating, 126

send back food in a restaurant, 146

serrano pepper, 126

shellfish, *see* crawfish, lobster,
    oysters

snails, 26

soup, 92

soup bowl, 83

soup spoon, 82

soybeans, 44

"specials" on the menu, 118

spicy food, 124

split a restaurant bill, 114

spoons, types of, 82

stemless wineglass, 96

stemware, *see* glasses, wineglass

stilton cheese, 88

stone fruit, 42

sushi, 108

T

table setting, 80

tea, 104

Thai chili pepper, 126

tip, 111

toast (as speech), 101

tongue burn, 144

trotters, 74

V

vegetarian, 132

W

walnuts, 64, 65

whole fish, 12

wine, 94, 98

wineglass, 95. *See also* glasses

World's Hottest Pepper, 126

ACKNOWLEDGMENTS

Thanks to my agent, Sally Ekus, who saw the power in a single tweet. Thanks for helping me make my childhood dream of seeing my name in print come true!

Thanks, Mom, for encouraging my writing and always supporting me, even when most parents would balk at their kid going to school for creative writing.

And thank you to Jane Yolen for giving me an award in writing way back in first grade. You made my little kid ego soar and I haven't looked back since.

Thank you to my awesome editor, Tiffany Hill, for guiding me through my first book and generally being awesome. #MillennialPower!